GLIMPSES OF PRE-SOCRATIC PHILOSOPHERS

Through Brief Qs & As

V. V. Raman

ARIP

In the 1980s when I gave a ourse on Ancient Science and Scientists, I prepared for the students a series of simple questions and answers for preparing for the test. This was a simple way of reviewing the main points in the course. This is one from that series. The reader can learn about the Pre-Socratic philosophers who laid the foundations for Science in the Western world.

CONTENTS

I

PRE-SOCRATIC PHILOSOPHERS

1 Who are the pre-Socratics?

The philosophers of ancient Greece that we have considered in the previous sections are generally referred to as the pre Socratics as they made their impact before the arrival of the great philosopher Socrates on the scene. Some historians of Greek philosophy, like J. Burnet, for example do not include Democritus in the list. It is generally accepted that the writings and ideas of the pre-Socratic philosophers were the starting point of the scientific worldview such as we understand and practice today.

2 How has our view of the pre-Socrates changed in the course of the 20th century?

It used to be thought that the Ionian philosophers were all of the opinion that there is a single reality which manifests itself in different forms; that this differentiation occurs because of modifications of the underlying substratum of matter, which was taken to be water, or apeiron or air or fire by different philosophers. This interpretation arose mainly from the writings of Aristotle. But the current view among scholars is different. Now it is believed that rather than start with an all embracing picture of physical reality, the Greek thinkers took the world to be made up of a large number of individual entities. This change in perspective has given rise to considerable scholarly re-interpretation of pre-Socratic Greek thought. It must, however, be pointed out that not all scholars agree with the newer interpretations. Also, for practical purposes of forming a general idea of what the various philosophers of antiquity said and wrote, the more simplistic picture, arising from Aristotle's accounts, are adequate.

3. How has the pre-Socratic period of Greek philosophy been described to emphasize its significance in the history of science?

In his *History of the Inductive Sciences* (1837) W. Whewell wrote: "The sages of early Greece form the heroic age of science. Like the first navigators in their own mythology, they boldly ventured their untried bark in a distant and arduous *voyage*, urged by the hopes of a supernatural success; and though they missed the imaginary golden prize which they sought, they un locked the gates of distant regions, and opened the seas to the keels of the thousands of adventurers, who, in succeeding times, sailed to and fro, to the infinite increase of the mental treasures of mankind." This passage was taken as an inspiration for a book, entitled *The Heroic Age of Science,* by W.A. Heidel (1933). Extending his discussions beyond the pre-Socratic period Heidel showed how the ingredients of the modern scientific framework may be found in the ideals, conceptions and methodology of the ancient Greeks. One should not forget the context in which the Greek scientific spirit emerged. As expressed by G.E.R. Lloyd, "The essence of the Milesian contribution was to introduce a new critical spirit into man's attitude to the world of nature, but this should be seen as a counterpart to, and offshoot of, the contemporary development of the practice of free debate and open discussion in the context of politics and law throughout the Greek world." (*Early Greek Science: Thales to Aristotle*, p.15)

4 What can we say about the historical scholarship in this field?

There has been an impressive amount of historical scholar ship in the field of pre-Socratic philosophy and science. New insights and points of view have been gained on the subject during our own century. In the words of one scholar in the field, "No other field offers as inviting a challenge to the philosophical imagination, yet in as demanding an environment of evidential and interpretive controls. Standards of precision are high, methodological issues have often been aired, a repertoire of alternative interpretations is already on record, and there is a firmly established tradition of doing justice not only to the primary texts but to ancient and modern commentary as well. At least within the last one hundred years, discussion within the field has been remarkably continuous and cumulative, and progressively more sensitive to the nuances, levels, or strata, as well as the presuppositions and repercussions, of philosophic argument. ..." (A.P.D. Mourelatos, *The Pre-Socratics*, p.3.)

II

THALES OF MILETUS

1. Who is generally regarded as the first ancient Greek scientists?

Thales (625 BCE - 547 BCE) of Miletus is generally referred to as the first philosopher and scientist in Western civilization. Aristotle called him the Founder of Philosophy.

2. Who are some of the ancient writers from whom we have gained our knowledge of Thales and of other early Greek scientists?

Modern historians owe a great deal to many writers of ancient times who have left for us comments and anecdotes pertaining to the most early thinkers whose original writings are lost. Among the major ancient writers who have served us well in this regard we may mention Herodotus, Diogenes Laertius, Aristotle, and Plutarch and Theophrastus.

3. Who was Herodotus?

Herodotus was a Greek historian: perhaps the very first of all historians. His writings have provided us with a fund of information on various aspects of ancient peoples and cultures. They were based on his own extensive travels. Herodotus lived in the 5th century BCE The word history derives from the Greek word *istorie* which means simply inquiry. Herodotus used the word in its modern connotation of inquiry into the past. It is said that he read his history to the public in Athens and in Olympia.

Herodotus also realized how difficult it is to be certain about one's statements in writing history. "My business is to record what people say," he is reputed to have remarked, "but I am not obliged to believe it all."

4 Who was Diogenes Laertius?

Diogenes Laertius was a Greek author who lived in the 3rd century A.D. He has left a history of Greek thought which has been widely used by modern writers to gather information on ancient thinkers. His work, translated as *Lives and Opinions of Eminent Philosophers*, was first published in the English version in 1853. Although Diogenes presents us with a veritable sourcebook of interesting information, he is not always reliable. Yet, the mere fact that he has left for posterity some records of the lives and sayings of ancient thinkers is valuable enough. This is what prompted Michel de Montaigne to wish there had been not one, but a dozen Diogenes Laertius.

5 Who was Aristotle?

Aristotle (384 BCE - 324 BCE) was the scientist-philosopher par excellence of ancient Greece. His influence on Western thought has hardly been equaled, although the rise of modern science in the 17th century demanded an abandoning of Aristotle's worldviews. He too, in his writings, made numerous references to previous Greek thinkers.

6 Who was Plutarch?

Plutarch (46 A.D. - 120 A.D.) was yet another Greek writer. His book, *Parallel Lives (Bioi Paralleloi)* is a compendium of brief biographies of famous Greek and Roman personages. Though most of his subjects are from the field of politics and the military, there are enough references to eminent philosophers in the work for it to be of interest to the historian of Greek science.

7 Who was Theophrastus?

Theophrastus (371 BCE - 287 BCE) was an associate of Aristotle, who did work on botany and philosophy. But he also wrote several histories of science in ancient Greece. His work led to a classification of ancient thinkers based on their opinions. This classification is referred to as the doxographical tradition. This is a primary source of information for the historian of Greek philosophy. The eminent German scholar Hermann Alexander Diels (1848 - 1922) systematized the numerous material on this subject in 187

8 What specific achievement of Thales is said to have brought him great fame?

According to Herodotus, on one occasion, when the hostile armies of the Lydians and the Persians stood face to face to begin a battle, a solar eclipse that Thales had predicted came to pass. This is said to have occurred on May 28, 585 BCE The warring kings are said to have made peace right away, and they even entered into some matrimonial alliance. This made Thales famous.

9 What, according to an older view, was the basis for Thales' prediction?

It used to be thought that Thales was aware of the Baby Ionian Saros which referred to the period between eclipses, and that Thales himself had observed the Egyptian solar eclipse of 603 BCE From these he calculated the year when the solar eclipse in question would take place. This explanation was accepted for a long time. The idea of the Babylonian saros was put forward by Edmund Halley in 1691.

10 On what basis do we know that the 'Thales eclipse' occurred exactly on May 28, 585 BCE?

From Herodotus' account and other historical data one
could only surmise that the said eclipse took place sometime between 625 BCE and 583 BCE It was during the mid-19th century that several scholars investigated this question with pains taking research. In particular, the efforts of J. R. Hind and G. B. Airy in the 1850's led to the determination of the exact date. On the other hand the work of G. Smith seemed to establish that the Babylonians were aware of the periodicity of eclipses.

11 How has this explanation been challenged?

More meticulous examination of ancient records by 0. Neugebauer has led to the view that the Babylonians did not have such precise knowledge of the saros as Halley had suggested. In his classic work, *Exact Sciences of Antiquity* (1952), Neugebauer analyzed ancient mathematics and astronomy, of Babylonia, and Egypt, as well as their influence on Greek thought. His conclusion was that Thales had no previous knowledge of Babylonian science when he made the prediction: indeed that during the time of Thales the Babylonians probably did not themselves have any knowledge of the saros as Halley had said. Quite possibly Thales merely made a rough prediction which, by sheer chance, turned out to be very close to the correct date. Or again, after the occurrence of the eclipse Thales could have claimed that his prediction had been just what was observed. And as he was a respected scholar the common folk would have readily believed him. This, at any rate, is the current explanation accepted by most scholars, such as, for example, Sarton.

12 Who was George Sarton?

George Sarton (1884 - 1956) was one of the most outstanding historians of science of our times. His dedication to historical research in the field of science and his tireless efforts to foster greater interest in this subject were largely responsible for molding science history into a separate academic discipline. Aside from his major work, *Introduction to the History of Science* (First Volume: 1927), his most memorable legacy is the founding of the journal ISIS in 1912. This is the official journal of the *History of Science Society*. This international journal is "devoted to the history of science and its cultural influences."

13. What was Thales' view of the earth?

Thales imagined the earth to be a flat disk floating on a sea.

14. What is the famous saying attributed to Thales?

All things are water (*panta udor esti*). In other words, he declared that the entire material universe arose from water. This statement was attributed to Thales by Aristotle.

15. What might have prompted Thales to make such a declaration?

It is impossible for us to be sure of what inspired Thales to the idea. But historians have suggested possible reasons for his choice of water as the primordial substance. In Egypt and Babylonia, which were river based societies, and Thales' acquaintance with their cultures could have been a source of inspiration. His own observation of the abundance of water and its peculiar properties (the only substance that visibly changes states in nature) could have led him to recognize it as some thing unique, hence fundamental. Or again, the association of all life forms with water and moisture could well have suggested to Thales the importance of water. Some have seen in Thales choice of water (*whose* principal component is hydrogen: thus the proton) an instance of extraordinary scientific prescience!

16. What was Thales' concept of a magnet?

Apparently, again according to Aristotle, Thales believed that magnets, because they have the attractive property, must have a soul. This suggests that as early as the 5th century the basic property of magnets was known.

17. What are some mathematical theorems attributed to Thales?

Thales is credited with a knowledge and discovery of the following geometrical theorems :

(a) The diameter of a circle bisects it.

(b) The base angles of an isosceles triangle are equal.

(c) Vertically opposite angles at the point of intersection of two straight lines are equal.

(d) The angle in a semi-circle is a right angle.

(e) The base and the angles at the base determine a triangle fully.

18. What is the current scholarly opinion as to the origin of Thales' mathematics?

According to the Greek writer Eudemus of Rhodes, Thales acquired his knowledge of geometry from Egypt. On the other hand, Van der Waerden traces Babylonian influences in Thales' mathematics. Neugebauer maintains that neither Egyptian nor Babylonian mathematics of the time of Thales was advanced enough to have served as sources for Thales' mathematics. And W. K. C. Guthrie reminds us that "even if we has unimpeachable statements

in ancient authorities that Thales proved this or that theorem, the word 'proof' has a meaning only in relation to its historical context."

19 Who was Eudemus of Rhodes?

Eudemus, who lived in the 4th century BCE, was a student of Aristotle. Although he wrote works on philosophy and physics, his great contribution was his trilogy: History of Arithmetic, History of Geometry, and History of Astronomy. The original books of

Eudemus have not survived, but numerous references to them exist in the works of other ancient writers. As far as is known he was probably the very first historian of science, certainly the first to have written works explicitly entitled, History of ... a particular branch of science.

20 Who was Van der Waerden?

B. L. van der Waerden was an eminent Dutch historian of mathematics whose classic work (English translation), *Science Awakening* (1954) traces the early history of mathematics.

21 Who was W. K. C. Guthrie?

W. K. C. Guthrie was the British scholar and historian whose five-volume work, *History of Greek Philosophy* (1963-1970) is perhaps the most extensive and readable work on ancient Greek science and philosophy. Including an extensive bibliography, this work also discusses with clarity and scholarship the many controversies that have arisen among investigators of ancient science on problems of interpretation and critical analysis.

22 What was Plato's story about the absent-mindedness of Thales?

In one of his dialogues (Theaetetus) Plato tells the following story: Once Thales was walking in the fields observing the skies, and he slipped into a well. A servant girl saw this, and made fun of the philosopher's plight: though supposedly knowledgeable about the heavens, he was unable to see what was right here, down below!

23 What was Aristotle's story about the practical-mindedness of Thales?

Aristotle, in his *Poetics*, says the following story: Through his knowledge of astronomy Thales foresaw that there would be a rich olive harvest one particular year: whereupon he hired at a very low price all the oil presses in Miletus and Chios during wintertime when no one else was interested in them. And when harvest season came, he leased the presses at arbitrary prices. Thales thus proved, according to Aristotle, "that it was easy for philosophers to be rich if they chose."

24 What is the significance of these stories about Thales, told by Plato and Aristotle?

One tries to emphasize how impractical and absent minded a true philosopher generally is, and the other tries to emphasize that if and when a man of wisdom is engaged in non-profitable things it is because of a conscious choice on his part, and that if he so wishes he too can make a lot of money. In any event these stories reflect the two-fold power of science: As an intellectual activity it can be very rewarding in itself, even if on occasions it appears to be practically useless and wasteful; yet scientific knowledge can be immensely fruitful also, if one chooses to find applications for it.

25 How did Thales measure the heights of some pyramids?

Thales is said to have determined the heights of pyramids by simply measuring the lengths of shadows of pyramids at the instant when the length of the shadow of a standing man was equal to his own height. From this he concluded that the pyramid height was also the same as the length of the corresponding shadow.

26 What, according to Thales, is the most difficult thing to do, and what is the easiest thing to do?

According to Diogenes Laertius, Thales is said to have remarked that to know oneself is the most difficult thing, and to give advice is the easiest thing to do.

27 Who were the Seven Wise Men of Greece?

Seven famous philosophers and legislators who lived during a time span of some seven decades (620 BCE - 550 BCE) came to be regarded as The Seven Wise Men (hoi hepta sophoi). The list sometimes varies from author to author, but invariably the name of Thales tops the list. Others, according to one version, included: Cleobulos of Rhodes, Bias of Priene, Pittacos of Mytilene, Solin of Athens, Epicharnos of Cos, and Anaxagoras of Clazomenae.

28 What is the significance of Thales in the history of physics?

Thales was perhaps the first person in the Western tradition to have attempted to reduce the variety in the material world to a single substance, viz. water. This effort to bring the complexity of the observed phenomena into a simple framework of one or a few all embracing entities has always been one of the major goals of the scientific enterprise. Thales was also the first known philosopher to have sought explanations in terms of material and physical causes, displaying very little inclination towards supernatural explanations. This is what led Burnet to describe science as "thinking about the world in the Greek way."

29 Who was John Burnet?

John Burnet (1863-1928) was an eminent Scottish classical scholar who wrote several works on Greek thinkers. His most memorable work, of relevance to those interested in Greek science, is the one entitled: *Early Greek Philosophy* (1892). In this is work, which includes quotations from many of the ancient philosophers, Burnet expounded on the thesis that the Greeks were the first to point out the way to science.

30. Where did Thales and the early Greek scientists thrive?

In Ionia, which is located in Western Asia Minor. Of the five main lines of migration from Greece, one was Ionian. By the 7th century BCE twelve major settlements were part of Ionia: Miletus, Myus, Priene, Ephesus, Kolophon, Lebedus, Teos, Erythrae,

Klazomenae, Phocaea, Samos, and Chios. Ionia consisted of a narrow mainland and several islands.

31 How does one account for the fact that science first arose in Ionia?

The origins of scientific thought and revolutions in science are difficult to account for. They constitute challenging problems for the historian of science. One older view regarding cultural and scientific creativity held that a particular people were gifted in special ways, that there are racially inherent qualities which facilitate the origin and development of science in certain demographic contexts and not in others. Both science and scholarship have revealed that uniqueness in matters of intellectual capacity is a mistaken and prejudiced notion which has no basis whatever on facts. (This is not to say that such views are no longer held by thinkers and non-thinkers alike.)

On the other hand, external factors in a society may be conducive or obstructive to the development of a people along new modes of thought. In the case of the Ionians, for example, the newly established colony had fresh political institutions. It was as yet a society where traditions and old customs were not stagnating the mind. Also, because of the thriving commerce with alien shores there was a continual intermingling of peoples with different interests and varied backgrounds. Such interactions always open up new ways of thinking and fresh modes of viewing problems. Moreover technical needs arose, and these instigated search for solutions to problems that had not arisen before. All this provided ample opportunities for eager investigation, serious reflection, and original thought.

32 In this context, how does Sarton draw parallels between Thales and Benjamin Franklin?

In his book *A History of Science* (Volume I), Sarton wrote: "Both (Thales and Franklin) were living in a stimulating environment, and both responded to it with open mind and natural genius. Both were inquisitive, quick to learn, ready to apply their knowledge to practical aims. Thales' journey to Egypt is like Franklin's to England; both observed eagerly what was done in the old World and brought back the notions that they deemed useful. Franklin brought back a knowledge of electricity and Thales that of astronomy.

III

ANAXIMANDER AND ANAXIMENES

1. Who was Anaximander?

Anaximander was a fellow citizen of Thales, hence a Milesian also. He was perhaps fifteen years younger than Thales and is believed to have been the latter's pupil.

2. Which is the work that is usually regarded as "the first treatise on natural philosophy in the history of mankind?"

Anaximander's book, *On the Nature of Things* (periphyseos). Unfortunately most of this work is lost. We find references to in first in Aristotle. Most ancient Greek philosophers wrote on this theme, and the title of the works were very often the same. It is interesting to note that Thales, generally regarded the first scientist and philosopher, is not known to have written any book!

3. How did he modify Thales' teaching as to the ultimate origin of all material things?

Anaximander felt that water could not be the ultimate substance, indeed that the existence of water itself needs to be explained. In his view the material universe arose from something that is not as tangible as any of the commonly experienced substances. He introduced the word apeiron to describe this prime substance. The term would be translated as that which is infinite or boundless or indefinite. Apeiron, he maintained, is the arche or principle or beginning of everything.

4. What is regarded as (one of) the earliest statements of a law of nature?

The first statement in Anaximander's book which reads: "That from which all things are born is also the cause of their coming to an end, as it is meet, for they pay reparations and atonement to each other for their mutual injustice in order of time." Western historians of science often refer to this as the first full statement of a law of nature. Similar statements may be found in earlier writings in other cultures, such as in the Rig Veda of India which dates back to over a thousand years before Christ. However, such writings are usually inspired by mystical or 'mythical' perspectives, and do not embody the purely naturalistic attitude of the Milesians.

5. What was Anaximander's theory of cosmogony?

Anaximander imagined that in the beginning a seed of hot and cold was separated away from the eternal, boundless apeiron, and that thence emerged a huge sphere of flame around the air, like the bark of a tree. This is regarded as one of the first naturalistic explanations for the origin of the universe.

6. What was Anaximander's insight on the existence of opposites?

Anaximander was one of the first early Greek thinkers to recognize the role of opposite pairs of entities in the world : hot and cold, wet and dry, life and death, etc. Anaximander sought to understand the world in terms of the conflicts between such opposites.

7. What was Anaximander's picture of the earth?

Anaximander's earth has been compared to a stone column. He pictured the earth as a cylinder. According to Theophrastus the ratio of the diameter to height in Anaximander's cylindrical earth was as (?) But the most significant idea in Anaximander's view is that for the first time in the history of human thought the earth did not need any support to be in the universe.

8. What was another 'first' that Anaximander is credited with?

In the words of the geographer Agathemerus, "Anaximander of Miletus, the pupil of Thales, was the first to depict the inhabited earth on a chart." In other words, he made the first map of the world. His map was circular, with Hellas in the central region, and Delphi at the center of Hellas.

9. What was a profound scientific insight that Anaximander is said to have had?

A concept of evolution in the biological world. Anaximander is said to have expressed the view that man probably arose from lower, aquatic animals. More exactly he seems to have held the view that once upon a time human embryos were formed within fish-like creatures whence they came out as human beings.

10. What can we say for certain about Anaximander as a man?

Practically nothing. In spite of the fact that a trunkless ancient statue bearing Anaximander's name has survived we know very little about him as a man; much less even than about Thales. As C. H. Kahn stated, "Anaximander stands ... as a symbol such opposites for the anonymous creative spirit of Ionian thought in the sixth century. The personal features of Anaximander's life and speculation are as completely mutilated for us as is the trunkless remnant of an archaic statue from Miletus which bears his name."

11. Where does Kahn make this statement?

C. H. Kahn makes this comment in his scholarly study entitled, *Anaximander and the Origins of Greek Cosmology* (1960). This is an excellent example of a technical work in (Greek) science history, based on numerous original sources and scholarly papers and controversies. In this work Kahn makes the following assessment of Anaximander: "As one examines the remains of this early period, it is

Anaximander who emerges more and more clearly as the central figure in sixth century thought. It is, in all probability, his work that laid down the lines along which ancient science was to develop and his mind which gave the Greek philosophy of nature its characteristic stamp.... It was he who first wrote down his views *periphyseos* (on the nature of things), and thereby established a new literary form - the first in which prose was employed- which *was* to serve as the written basis for the new scientific tradition. His work is thus the ancestor of all later specimens of the genre..."

12. Who was Anaximenes?

Anaximenes was the third of the great Milesian thinkers. He was junior to Anaximander, and probably died around 526 BCE He is said to have written "in the pure unmixed Ionian dialect."

13. What was Anaximenes' *arche*? i.e. his view on the ultimate source of all matter?

As Thales had talked of water and Anaximander of the apeiron, Anaximenes took pneuma (air) as being the ultimate substance. He imagined air to be made up of tiny particles, and said that when air condenses, we get water, earth and other substances; whereas when it undergoes rarefaction, we get fire.

14. on what basis did Anaximenes arrive at this conclusion?

It is said that Anaximenes observed the different effects of breathing out, with almost fully closed lips and with fairly well opened mouth. In the first case one gets cool air, in the second, the air is warm. These observations led him to his theory

15. What new idea is introduced in Anaximenes' theory of condensation and rarefaction?

The idea that quantitative factors (degree of condensation or rarefaction) have effects on qualitative changes (becoming water or fire). This was a major conceptual advance.

15. What was Anaximenes' idea of God?

Anaximenes felt that the pneuma of the entire world constitutes God. And the whole world breathes also.

16. What, according to Sarton, is the significance of this view?

In developing the idea that the entire world is breathing Anaximenes was extending his individual experiences to a universal possibility. This, says, Sarton, is the drawing of a parallel which links the "little world" with the "big world." Such an effort was the first of many in the centuries to follow.

17. What was Anaximenes theory of the rainbow?

Anaximenes is said to have given the following explanation for the rainbow: "The rainbow is produced when the beams of the sun fall on thick condensed air. Hence the anterior Part of it seems red, being burnt by the sun's rays, while the other part is dark, owing to the predominance of moisture." Once again, the importance of this lies in that fact that an attempt was rnade to give a naturalistic explanation for an observed phenomenon.

18. What was the impact of Anaximenes?

According to Sarton, the impact of Anaximenes was considerable. i:n his view Anaximander and Thales were soon forgotten and when one spoke of Milesian philosophy, one referred to Anaximenes. But according to Kahn, it was Anaximander who emerges as the central figure in the 6th century (see

19. How do we reconcile this with Sarton's view in 18?

This is not surprising. When it comes to assessment and evaluation, historians of science have sometimes held very divergent views on many issues. So this difference in opinion as to who had a greater impact is no exception in historica1 scholarship. History never judges, but historians always do.

20. What may be said in general terms about the Milesian school of philosophers?

Thales, Anaximander, and Anaximenes. were the three great philosophers of Miletus. They were also the first thinkers in the Western world to reflect upon the physical phenomena in naturalistic terms. They were thus the ones who laid the foundations for what we call the scientific approach to the world around us. They inherited the mythologies of former generations and were surely enriched by the ideas and points of view tha.t had developed in other great civilizations. But their originality in formulating new questions and from different perspectives was considerable.

It is perhaps an exaggeration to say that science began with Thales in Miletus, but it is quite fa.ir to note that the perennial quest for understanding and explaining the physica,1 world – which is what the scientific enterprise is all about- received more than a significant boost from the first philosophers of Miletus; and this was to have a. lasting impact on the future course of history. The rational approach of the Milesians, and their materialistic cosmologies did not mean that they did not think in terms of souls and spirits. In fact their view often was that everything in nature was imbued with some spirit. Indeed this is what gave rise to their view of nature as something that tends to grow and evolve, much like a living organism. It is such a nature that they had in mind when they used the word *psysis* which has given rise to *our* own term Physics.

IV
PYTHAGORAS

1. Who was Pythagoras?

Pythagoras (560 BCE - 480 BCE) of Samos was a mathematician and mystic thinker who, after many travels, founded a brotherhood at Croton in southern Italy. The Pythagorean school had great influence on the thought modes of several generations.

2. What do we know about the life of Pythagoras?

We know *very* little with any certainty about this remarkable character in science history. Yet a great deal of interesting legend has grown around his name. And where certainty is impossible it is sometimes interesting to recall the legends. Pythagoras is said to have traveled widely, certainly to Egypt and possibly to still more distant lands, including India. Pythagoras also left his native Samos which had come under the rule of a tyrant by the name of Polycrates, and settled down in the Greek colony of Croton. Here he founded his famous school, and here he also helped the government formulate a new constitution. Pythagoras is also credited with the introduction of a new coinage in Croton. With all that, Pythagoras finally provoked much dislike and reaction against him from various sections of people in Croton, as much because of his ultra-conservatism as because of the secrecy which characterized his brotherhood. Uprisings against the Pythagoreans ensued in which several members of the group were ruthlessly murdered. Pythagoras himself was exiled, and the old man past seventy five *years* of age is saidto have gone into a temple where he died eventually as a result of not having eaten for many days.

3. What does the so-called Pythagorean Theorem in geometry say?

In a right-angled triangle, the square on the hypotenuse is equal to the sum of the squares on the other two sides. Thus, if the two son-hypothenuse sides of a right-triangle are 3 and 4 units, the hypotenuse will be 5 units: $3^2 + 4^2 = 5^2$.

4. What were the subjects that Pythagoras and his followers studied?

The Pythagoreans were primarily interested in four subjects: arithmetic, geometry, music, and astronomy.

5. What is the origin of the word mathematics?

Originally the word *mathematike* simply meant any *learning* (Even *now* the word *polymath* refers to a person who is learned in many fields.) And it *was* the Pythagoreans who first used the word in the sense of a study of arithmetic and geometry particularly, whence its modern connotation.

6. How were the students of the Pythagorean school subdivided?

Students in the Pythagorean school were divided into two large groups: the outer students (*exoterici* or *acusmatici*) who were given only the summaries of the various teachings of the master, without too many explanations (not unlike non-science majors taking courses like 'Physics for Poets'); and the inner students (*esoterici* or *mathematici*) who were initiated into the details and secrets of the master's wisdom. Another way of
looking at this classification is to regard the acusmatici as those interested primarily in the religious aspects of Pythagorean teaching, and the mathematics as those interested in the mathematical-physical aspects.

7. What were some of the beliefs and taboos of the Pythagoreans?

They Pythagoreans were vegetarians and teetotalers. They were forbidden to laugh. They were not allowed to walk on highways, nor touch a white cock. They believed in the transmigration of souls. Most important of all, they were ordered never to eat any beans!

8. What inspired these and similar practices?

The Pythagoreans were essentially a magic-minded lot. They believed in symbols and portents, and generally subscribed to a great many superstitions. They were mystical and secretive, and really thought they interacted with nature in mysterious ways. They thought, for example, that beans enclose the souls of dead people, hence can develop into weird forms if buried for long in dung.

9. What was the underlying thesis of the Pythagorean worldview?

Pythagoras taught that the essence of all things is numbers.

One can always find numbers in everything, concrete or abstract. Thus they assigned numbers to people, to animals, to events, and to activities. The number corresponding to an animal, for example, would be the number of stones required to make an outline of its form. The modern pseudo-science of numerology goes back to the Pythagoreans.

10. What was' Pythagoras' Divine Music theory?

Although one has to rely only on various secondary and tertiary sources and quotations, one generally credits the Pythagoreans with the discovery that the production of harmonious sounds is related to specific ratios of the lengths of vibrating strings. Pythagoras is believed to have recognized that the ratios 1:2, 3:2 and 4:3 correspond to the basic intervals of (Greek) music. When the string lengths in a musical instrument are as 12:9:8:6, harmonious sounds result. This discovery of a quantitative law pertaining to sound entitles Pythagoras to be regarded as the founder of the science of acoustics.

11. How did Pythagoras extend this discovery?

Recognizing that the numbers 1, 2, 3 and 4 which are involved in the harmony relationships add up to 10, Pythagoras felt that this reflected a certain order and beauty in the world. This order and beauty in the *world* around were described by him as *kosmos*, which is the origin of the later scientific concept of the cosmos.

12. How was the number mysticism extended to heavenly bodies?

The Pythagoreans believed that when heavenly bodies move, probably with speeds much greater than bodies on earth, they too much produce sounds. These sounds must be all the greater since those bodies are so much more massive. They also discerned some ratios between the distances of heavenly bodies. Although how they accomplished this is quite a mystery, Eudemus informs us that the Pythagoreans were indeed the ones who investigated the relative planetary distances for the first time. In any event, from the discovery of simple ratios here also they concluded that there must exist harmonious sounds in the heavens because of the motions of the heavenly bodies.

13. How did they account for the fact that we do not hear any such heavenly music?

The Pythagoreans believed that as we are subjected to that heavenly sound right from the moment of birth we are totally unaware of its presence. Sound becomes perceptible, they held, only in opposition to silence. The bronze smith often does not hear the noise he is making because he has become so much accustomed to it. They believed, however, that Pythagoras himself could clearly hear the music of the spheres.

14. What was Pythagoras' conception of the earth?

Pythagoras is said to have believed that the earth is spherical and that it is rotating. These were certainly remarkable discoveries, made apparently, not on the basis of any detailed observations, but by conjecture and speculation.

15 What was the model of the universe that the Pythagoreans accepted?

The Pythagoreans believed that the earth and the other planets (including the sun) revolved around a central fire which is forever invisible to us since we are always facing away from it. There is also, they said, another earth, a sort of mirror image to ours, which too is revolving about the central fire. Although this is not quite the Copernican (heliocentric) view, this was the first instance of the idea of a non-geocentric universe. What is even more remarkable is that, if we picture the center of our galaxy to be the Pythagorean central fire, Pythagoras was even closer to the modern view than Copernicus. Also, the counter-earth idea of Pythagoras has a faint resemblance to the particle-antiparticle notion of modern physics.

16. What was Pythagoras' theory of vision?

Pythagoreans are said to have believed that small particles emanated from objects that are visible to us, and that these enter the eye and make us see things.

17. What was Pythagoras' view of the relevance of mathematics?

Pythagoras is said to have held the view that numbers are relevant to ordinary people only in so far as they serve useful purposes in matters of everyday concern: such as measuring and counting. But, he maintained, there are profound truths hidden behind numbers, great secrets of nature which the inquiring mind alone can comprehend. Thus Pythagoras was one of the first to recognize the relevance of mathematics in physics.

18. Did Pythagoras discover the Theorem of Pythagoras?

The modern answer to this question is, No. The Babylonians had a knowledge of the basic property of the sides of a right angled triangle centuries before Pythagoras. An ancient tablet of Sumerian origin, dating back to almost 2000 years before Christ, has been found indicating a knowledge of the theorem. Neugebauer has shown that the so-called Pythagorean Theorem was probably acquired by Pythagoras from the Babylonians.

19. What was the attitude of the Pythagoreans to knowledge?

The Pythagoreans had almost emotional attachment to know ledge and wisdom. They regarded as the goal of life, not simply wisdom (*sophia*), but the love of wisdom (*philosophia*). Thus Pythagoras was also the originator of the concept of philosophy in the Western tradition.

20. In what ways did Pythagorean thinking differ from the thinking of the Milesian philosophers?

Originally Pythagoras was an Ionian himself, born as he was in Samos. And he is also reported (by Iamblichos) to have met Thales of Miletus. Yet his thinking was quite different from that of the Milesian philosophers. The Milesians were matter-of-fact thinkers whose ideas tended towards materialism. The Pythagoreans, on the other hand, were mystic-minded, religious, spiritual and tended to be obscurantist. The Milesians were primarily interested in the qualitative features of the world. The Pythagoreans probed into quantitative relations, indeed they were obsessed by numbers. And both have had their impacts in different ways on the development of science. The one has given rise to the rationalistic and materialistic component of science; and the other to the mystical and mathematical components.

21. Was Pythagoras influenced by Indian thought?

In the course of the 19th century some scholars believed that Pythagoras had indeed traveled to India and possibly even to China whence he assimilated his notions on the transmigration of souls, pairs of opposites, vegetarianism, etc. The eminent historian of Greek philosophy and theologian Eduard Zeller (1814 - 1908), however, challenged that thesis, and the view of a scholar like L. von Schroeder to the effect that there are indeed discernible Indian influences in Pythagorean thought has been dismissed by most Western historians of science, although it is still usual to refer to mystical and obscurantist scientific approaches among the Greeks as "oriental influences." Western scholars of the period usually have three kinds of answers to a question of this type.

Either they suggest the possibility that similar ideas developed independently in India and in Greece, or they assert that it was Greece that influenced Indian thought, or they remain fairly non-committal. Even such an erudite historian as Guthrie who wrote five extensive volumes on Greek philosophy has only this to say on this question: "Whether the parallels with Indian thought originate from a common Indo-European heritage is a question which, if it admits of any answer at all, lies far beyond the scope of this study."

22. Which is a recent scholarly study of Pythagorean traditions as they have developed from the writings of Aristotle?

J. A. Philip's work *Pythagoras and Early Pythagoreanism* (1966), analyzes the many sources of Pythagorean tradition emerging from Aristotle's writings, and refutes most of the latter. The author calls into question the whole idea of the Pythagorean Brotherhood which has been accepted as an unquestionable fact over the centuries by all writers on Pythagoras.

In his final statement on Pythagoras Philip notes: "His (Pythagoras') importance in the history of philosophy is, in part, due to his theories of physical structure as numerically expressible and to his anticipation of quantitative analysis. These notions ... were an important influence on Greek speculation throughout antiquity. But yet more important was his conception, or the pattern he established, of philosophy as a way of life and an intellectual and spiritual discipline by means of which the soul progresses towards the actualization of its divine nature and towards knowledge."

V
HERACLITUS OF EPHESOS

1. What, in brief, were the origins of the material world, as proposed by the three Milesians, and what question remained unanswered in this context?

The Milesians proposed water (Thales), *apeiron* (Anaximander), and *pneuma* (Anaximenes) are the ultimate entities of all material things. The unanswered question was: Why do the ultimate things change to produce other things?

2. Who provided an answer to this question?

Heraclitus of Ephesos, who is known to have flourished about 500 BCE, explained the changes that occur in the physical world.

3. What was his explanation?

Heraclitus explained change in terms of his doctrine of *Opposite Tension*. According to this, everything is characterized by the coexistence in it of opposite tendencies, Usually these are balanced. But the balance can be easily upset when one of the forces gets the upper hand.

Then the equilibrium is spoiled, and changes occur. He did not attach value judgments to the opposites, as good and bad, for example. In fact, he maintained that such opposing principles can be helpful.

4. What was Heraclitus' concept of the unity of opposites?

Heraclitus further maintained that the apparent opposites are intrinsically the same, and only seem to be different. One example he gave of this was the 'up' and 'down' of a road, which appear to be different only because of the different perspectives, but essentially refer to the same property of the road. The co existence of opposites gives rise to symmetrical phenomena, like day and night, summer and winter, etc.

5. What, according to Heraclitus, is the root of everything, the ultimate element?

The ultimate *arche*, according to Heraclitus, is Fire. In his own words, the world is "made neither by a god nor by man, but it was, and is, and shall be, ever-living Fire, in measures being kindled and in measures going out." Scholars have argued endlessly about the significance and interpretation of this statement. The essential idea is that one the one hand we find fire being generated and extinguished all over the world and at all times; and on the other hand, it plays a subtle role in

the maintenance of the opposite tensions in things. The idea of an ever-living Fire suggests that Heraclitus meant by the word something more than the usual physical fire we are accustomed to, and perhaps meant equally the vital-fire, the life principle itself. Indeed, as D. F. Furley has suggested, Heraclitus most probably "meant to use fire as a paradigm for explaining (some or all) continuing natural processes: fire consumes things and changes them into itself, as smoke and hot vapor, and later there is condensation and re-formation of liquids and solids." (DSB: VI-290).

6. What is the most famous saying of Heraclitus?

Everything flows and nothing abides (*panta rhei ouden menei*). Heraclitus was the philosopher of change. He recognized that nothing is permanent in this world. Even the apparently permanent things are in fact changing, though extremely slowly. "You cannot step into the same river twice," is another saying of Heraclitus to express the same idea. From the alternation of night and day and of the seasons he also held the view that changes often occur from opposite to opposite.

7. What is the title of the book that Heraclitus is supposed to have written?

It is generally accepted that we have with us some authentic sayings of Heraclitus. Although some authors have suggested that Heraclitus did write some books, basing themselves for the most part on Diogenes Laertes' account, most modern scholars question this. G. S. Kirk, who has made scholarly studies on several of Heraclitus' supposed writings, seriously doubts that Heraclitus wrote any detailed book himself. This is the view he expresses in his *Heraclitus: the Cosmic Fragments* (1954).

According to Sarton, however, Heraclitus wrote a great book called on the Whole (peri tu pantos) which he deposited in the temple of Artemis.

8. Where can one find English translations of some of Heraclitus' sayings?

Statements attributed to Heraclitus were first assembled by F. Schleiermacher in 1817. Statements attributed to Heraclitus were also collected and published in 1877 by I. Bywater. An English translation of this work was published in 1889 by C.T.W. Patrick.

Burnet's book (A1.29) also have a number of Heraclitus' sayings.

9. What are some of Heraclitus' sayings?

The eyes are more exact witnesses than the ears.

All things are an exchange for Fire, and Fire for all things, even as *wares* for gold, and gold for wares.

Fire in its advance will judge and convict all things. The sun is new *every* day.

Men do not know how what is at variance agrees with itself. It is an attunement of opposite tensions, like that of the bow and the lyre.

Asses would rather have straw than gold.

Physicians who cut, burn, stab, and rack the sick, demand a fee for it which they do not deserve to get.

To God all things are fair and good and right, but men hold some things wrong and some right.

In the circumference of a circle the beginning and end are common.

It rests by changing.

Thought is common to all.

The mysteries practiced by men are unholy mysteries.

10. Where was one find a discussion of Heraclitus' sayings and a discussion of them?

P. Wheelwright's book, *Heraclitus* (1959), presents a detailed discussion of 124 sayings of Heraclitus. It also includes a long bibliography on Heraclitus. Wheelwright notes: "The ultimate reality, of which Heraclitus is trying to speak, cannot be adequately represented wither by a rationalistic concept such as 'being' or 'truth,' or by a theological concept such as 'Zeus' or 'God,' or by a naturalistic concept such as 'fire' or 'storms.' No word or image or idea can do it justice; but one of the least inadequate ways of symbolizing it, indicating as it does both its interrelating power and its elusiveness, is the phrase that Heraclitus employs - the hidden harmony."

11 What do we know about Heraclitus as a man?

It is said that Heraclitus was a haughty person in that he had only the utmost contempt for other people, including some the great philosophers of the age. He is reported to have declared that the poet Homer must be whipped. He described the philosophy of Pythagoras as nothing but an art of mischief. He himself believed that he had some revealed truths, that he was in fact a prophet.

12 How did Heraclitus die?

C. Bakewell, in his *Sourcebook in Ancient Philosophy* (1909), gives the following account, based in Diogenes Laertius' book: In this old age Heraclitus used to wander alone in the mountains, eating grasses and plants. He became sick as a consequence, and asked some medical men, as a riddle, whether they could cause draught after wet weather. But nobody could make out what he meant. This prompted him to "shut himself up in a stable for oxen, and cover himself with cow dung, hoping to cause the wet to evaporate from him by the warmth that this produced. And as he did himself no good in this way, he died, having lived seventy years."

VI

THE ELEATIC PHILOSOPHERS

1. What does one mean by the Eleatic philosophers?

Elea was a Phocaea colony in southern Italy which was founded
in the 530's B.C. The philosophers who flourished there are known as the Eleatic philosophers. Their ideas developed as a reaction to the Ionian school. Rather than accept a primary substratum for all matter (Milesians) and perpetual change (Heraclitus), they tried to picture a universal principle or being as the source of everything, and argued for perpetual no-change. The founder of the Eleatic school is said to have been inspired by Xenophanes.

2. Who was Xenophanes?

Xenophanes (c 580 B.C - 478 B.C.) pf Colophon was born in
Ionia, but traveled widely, and is said to have been involved with the founding of Elea. He was a poet and polemical writer who had a great influence on several philosophers of the time.

3. What was Xenophanes' theological position?

Xenophanes rejected anthropomorphic Gods. He propounded, instead, a single all-pervading divine principle that did not interfere in human affairs. He is said to have remarked: "There never was, nor ever will be, any man who knows with certainty the things about gods. ... Mortals fancy that gods are born, and wear clothes, and have voice and form like themselves. Yet if oxen and lions had hands, and could paint and fashion works as men do, they would make the pictures and images of gods in their own likeness…"

4. What is the relevance of Xenophanes in the history of science?

Although primarily a poet, Xenophanes had some profound scientific insights. He was one of the first philosophers to : consider earth as one of the basic elements. He gave interesting descriptions of fossils, and wrote on geological formations. He suggested, for example, that raised beaches resulted from layers of sea shells and marine fossils that had come inland. He believed the universe had always existed, and did not have a date of birth. He examined the limitations of human knowledge. Guthrie (A1.20) says: "The effect of his conception of knowledge as progressing steadily and gradually from small beginnings, through men's own powers of discove*ry* and invention, may be seen in many fifth century authors, both philosophers and poets..... With him philosophy breaks *new* ground in more than one direction, and sows new seed, from which a fruitful crop of ideas was soon to be reaped." Xenophanes is also regarded as one of the principal sources of the idealistic school of philosophy in the Western tradition. Plato regarded Xenophanes as the first of the Eleatic philosophers.

5. What was Xenophanes' view of the Pythagoreans?

He did not think much of them. In one of his poems he tells a story about Pythagoras stopping a friend from hurting a dog because, pleads Pythagoras, the dog was a re-incarnation of an old friend: a fact which Pythagoras could recognize from the familiar barking of the dog (which resembled the friend's voice)!

6. Who was Parmenides?

Parmenides (c 515 B.C - 450 BCE) of Elea was the greatest philosopher of the Eleatic school. He is believed to have studied with Pythagoras, but was much inspired by the writings of Xenophanes. Following perhaps the poet Xenophanes, Parmenides also wrote in verse, indeed the first of the philosophers to do so.

7. How did Parmenides's view differ from that of Heraclitus?

Heraclitus maintained that everything changes. Parmenides insisted that all things are one (hen ta panta); hence that there is essentially no change in the world.

8. How did Parmenides explain the changes and motions we actually observe in te world around us?

Parmenides said that the observed changes and motions are unreal. They result from our inability to recognize the essentially unchanging one that lies beneath all the apparent changes.

9. In which work did Parmenides expound his philosophy?

Parmenides expounded his philosophy in a ling poem entitled, as usual, *On Nature*. The poem has two parts which are called, *Way of Truth* and *Way of Opinion*. Only fragments of the poem have survived.

10. How did he explain the changes and motions we actually observe in te world around us?

Parmenides said that the observed changes and motions are unreal. They result from our inability to recognize the essentially unchanging one that lies beneath all the apparent changes.

11. What was Parmenides' attitude towards scientific inquiry in general?

In his poem *the Way of Truth* Parmenides wrote: "Turn your mind away from this (scientific) path of inquiry. Let not the habit engrained by manifold experience force you along this path, to make an instrument of the blind eye, the echoing ear, and the tongue, but test by reason my contribution to the debate."

12. What was Parmenides' contribution to the debate?

Parmenides' contribution to theoretical science was his emphasis on the value and power of pure logical reasoning in arriving at (purely speculative) results. (Aristotle called him the inventor of logic.) What Parmenides was suggesting was that instead of using the astronomical observations of planets and the Pythagorean investigations of sound, one should use logical
analysis.

13. Why was Parmenides against the Ionian philosophers in their efforts to establish positive sciences?

One consequence of Ionian science was a tendency to banish divinity from the scene. Parmenides was probably quite aware that atheism was gradually gaining ground. This was one reason why he attacked the scientific method of the Ionians. Other thinkers, in other ages, would develop similar attitudes for similar reasons in the course of science history.

14. Does the metaphysics of Parmenides have any relevance to the history of physics?

Although, superficially, much of Parmenides' writings are purely speculative and metaphysical, his views imply an understanding of some of the deeper problems of the philosophy of physics. A careful analysis of his writings led Santillana to the conclusion that Parmenides had a clear insight into the nature of mathematics and of physics. Santillana compared this to Einstein's appraisal of the matter when he (Einstein) declared: "If it is certain, it is not physics; if it is physics, it is not certain."

15. Who was Girogio de Santillana?

Giorgio de Santillana (1902 - 1974) was a scholar and historian of science who played a founding role in the School for the History of Science in Rome. He spent a good part of his life in the U.S., as Professor of History and Philosophy of Science at M.I.T. The particular analysis of Parmenides mentioned in A5.13 may be found in his book, The Origins of Scientific Thought: from Anaximander to Proclus, 600 BCE to A.D. 500.

16. What was the essential difference between the Ionian and the Parmenidean ways of interpreting physical reality?

The Ionians sought to explain the material universe in purely physical terms: using underlying elements (water, air) or a principle (apeiron). Parmenides asked more philosophically and abstractly, What is the meaning of existence or being? His answer was: Only what is, is; and what is not, is not. Therefore reality is complete, hence it does not change! It is this kind of reasoning that is characteristic of metaphysics. And it too has played a role in the development of scientific thought.

17. What exactly did Parmenides mean by statements like, 'what is, is," "what is not, is not"?

In Ionian thought there was a clear distinction between Being and Becoming. The idea was that there was one fundamental substratum, say water, and this transformed into, became, the multitude of other things. Parmenides objected to this. He maintained that when something is, it is there always. It does not become something else. Therefore all the so-called changes we observe are purely illusory, because what once was, always continues to be.

18. What kind of a world picture did he draw from this view?

According to Parmenides there is a plenum: filled space, in which, therefore, there can be no motion. The whole universe is one large, unchanging, unmoving, mass which remains forever the same. This is the ultimate reality. However, those who cannot and do not perceive this reality imagine all sorts of changes to be occurring in this world.

19 What was the significance of Parmenides in Greek philosophical thinking?

His views had a profound impact on later Greek thinkers. He showed the path of abstract thinking. Unfortunately his over emphasis on speculative thinking has had negative consequences also: in slowing down experimental and observational science. At the theory-making level, one began to think in terms of more than a single substratum, for only in this way could the multiplicity of experience be adequately accounted for.

20. Does Parmenides' idea of changes being mere illusions have any parallels in the history of ideas?

The Hindu concept of Máyá is very much the same. The Hindu metaphysicians also insisted that there is one unchanging under lying principle behind the phenomenal world, viz. Brahman, which alone is real. All the change and turmoil we see around us are purely illusory, resulting from our not perceiving that eternal One which is the Brahman. Interestingly enough, in ancient Hindu philosophical systems also there were two kinds of knowledge: Shruti or revealed knowledge, and Smriti or remembered knowledge, corresponding to Parmenides' Way of the Truth and Way of Opinion.

21. Where may one read more on Parmenides?

L. Taran's *Parmenides: A Text with Translation, Commentary, and Critical Essays* (1965) would be a good book to consult in this context. One may also look into W.J. Verdenius' *Parmenides: Some Comments on his Poem* (1942).

22 Who was the immediate successor of Parmenides as an Eleatic philosopher?

Zeno (490 BCE - 425 BCE) of Elea, who was a pupil of Parmenides, was the next great Eleatic philosopher. He extended Parmenides' logical methods to introduce paradoxes that result from certain assumptions. In other words, he introduced the practice of proving statements by means of *reductio ad absurdum*.

Zeno used this method, for example, to show that no change could occur in the world, and that there was only one reality: two propositions that his master had propounded.

23 What would be an example of Zeno's reasoning?

Zeno's proof that there is only one reality was given as follows: "If existences are many, they must be both alike and unlike: unlike inasmuch as they are not one and the same; and alike inasmuch as they agree in not being one and the same. But this is impossible, for unlike things cannot be alike, nor like things unlike. Therefore existences are not many."

24. What is Zeno's method of reasoning called?

It may be called dialectics: it is in fact the method by which one starts from the premises of an opponent, and by logical reasoning leading to absurdity, shows that the opponent's premises were wrong. Aristotle credited Zeno with the invention of the dialectic method.

25. How did Zeno apply his method to show that there is indeed no (empty) space?

Assuming that space is something in which some thing is, Zeno says: If there is space, it will be in some thing: for all that is, is in something, and that something is in space. So space will be in space, and so on ad infinitum. Therefore there is no space!

26. What are the two other famous paradoxes of Zeno?

1. *Achilles and the tortoise*. Achilles and the tortoise run a race. Achilles, the fast runner, can never overtake the tortoise which has a slight head start, because he must reach the point from where the tortoise started. By the time he

reaches that point, it has already moved on to another point. And by the time he reaches this second point, the tortoise has moved on to yet another point, and so on...

2. *An arrow in flight is at rest.* For, if everything is at rest when it occupies a space equal to itself, and that which is in flight at a given moment always occupies the space equal to itself, the arrow cannot move.

27. Wherein lies the solution to Zeno's paradoxes?

The resolution of Zeno's paradoxes involves a clear definition and understanding of the concepts of continuity and infinity in mathematics. Since these ideas were not refined until the development of modern mathematics and exploration of the foundations of mathematics, Zeno's paradoxes continued to confuse many intelligent thinkers over many generations.

28. What do we know about Zeno as a person?

Zeno is said to have been quite involved with the politics of Elea. According to Plato he wrote his work on paradoxes while still a young man, and did not really want to have them published. He was intent on proving the Pythagoreans wrong, and defended Parmenides against their attacks. According to Plato again, Zeno is said to have charged very high fees for his lectures. can be no motion.

29. How, according to Diogenes Laertius, did Zeno die?

Zeno was apparently involved in a plot to overthrow the tyrant Nearches who ruled Elea. The plot was unsuccessful. Zeno was caught, tortured, and killed. He is said to have died bravely.

30. How, then, can we summarize the difference in points of view between Heraclitus and the Eleatic philosophers?

This question may be answered in the words of Bertrand - Russel as follows: "The natural view to take of the world is that there are things which change: for example, there is an arrow which is now here, now there. The Eleatics said there were things but no changes. Heraclitus ... said there were changes but no things. The Eleatics said there was an arrow but no flight; Heraclitus ... said there was a flight but no arrow.

Each party conducted its argument by refutation of the other party. How ridiculous to say there is no arrow! say the "static" party. How ridiculous to say there is no flight! say the "dynamic" party...." (History of Western Philosophy, p.805)

31. Where can one read more on Zeno and his paradoxes?

Aside from H.D.P. Lee's *Zeno of Elea* (1936), one may consult the anthological work edited by W. C. Solomon and entitled, Zeno's Paradoxes. This work brings together many writings on the subject by philosophers of science, and includes a good portion on A. Grünbaum's book, *Modern Science and Zeno's Paradoxes.* As the editor points out, Zeno's paradoxes "have extensive ramifications both within philosophy and outside of it. ... They have deep significance for metaphysics and epistemology, but also occur on the borderline where philosophy must make positive contact with modern mathematics and physics. They constitute problems in the philosophy of science in the sense that their resolution demands that philosophy be made to bear upon science, and science upon philosophy...." (p. vii)

32 What non-Parmenidean inspiration has been attributed to Zeno's work?

Traditionally scholars have held the view, based primarily on Plato's writings, that Zeno was inspired to develop his ideas in defense of his master Parmenides whose ideas were ridiculed by his contemporaries. This view has been challenged by D.J. Furley. In his book, *Two Studies in the Greek Atomists* (1967), Furley analyzes the available documentations on the question and comes to the conclusion that Zeno was not so much trying to defend Parmenides as to answer some questions raised by Anaxagoras.

VII
EMPEDOCLES OF ARCAGAS

1. Who was the next great scientific thinker of the Italian (Greek) tradition?

Empedocles (492 BCE - 432 BCE) of Acragas is usually studied as the next great Greek thinker of the pre-Socratic era who flourished in the Italian colonies of Greece. Acragas is in Sicily, and during the time of Empedocles the city enjoyed great fame and power.

2. What is Empedocles famous for?

According to Aristotle, Empedocles was the one who introduced the idea of four basic roots or elements out of which the mate rial world is formed. Empedocles referred to the four roots as "Fire and water and earth and the immeasurable height of air." He refers to them as the roots of everything, and as the spring of mortal things. The variety of the physical world arise, he said, by the combination, in different proportions, of these *rhizomaten* (roots). All transformations of matter occur by the combination and splitting of substances.

3. What, according to Empedocles, brings about the combination and the splitting?

In addition to the passive factors of the four elements there are also in the world two active principles: love (*philotes*) and hate (*neikos*) or strife. These latter factors are responsible from bringing the elements together *or* breaking them apart.

4. What parallels may be drawn between this idea and modern ideas in physics?

There is an interesting parallel between Empedocles' concept and the modern concepts of particles and fields or interactions. In the current framework of physics the variety in the phenomenal world arises from the fundamental interactions that subsist among the fundamental particles. Also, the duality of interactions, of love and strife, corresponds to the possibility of attractive and repulsive forces in the physical world.

5. Did Empedocles envisage love and strife to be non-material forces as distinct from the material elements?

No. In his view the factors of love and strife were in fact embodied also. Aphrodite is the uniting force, for example. As Guthrie (A1.21) has pointed out, "Although Love and Strife are invisible and unimaginably fine and tenuous (more so, obviously, than air or fire), and although their influence is in the first place a psychological one, their spiritual character is not yet completely divorced from physical form.

6. What analogy can we draw to this idea with a concept in modern physics?

Interestingly, in modern particle physics also, one associates a particle (body) with every field. In other words, the forces of interaction are not entirely immaterial: they have a quantum aspect too, corresponding to the material aspects of love and hate in Empedocles' theory.

7. Where did Empedocles put forth his ideas?

Empedocles' scientific ideas are presented in a poem entitled, *On Nature* (*Peri physeis*) which is addressed to one of his students by the name of Pausanias. Indeed, Empedocles was the second of the scientists to compose his ideas in a poetic form. This is supposed to have been a very long poem, some 5000 lines in all, but just about 450 lines of it have survived. The work is repetitive on many matters. Another poetic work of Empedocles, called Purification (*kantharoi*) has also survived in parts.

8. What inspired Empedocles to imagine more than one fundamental element (root) in the physical world?

Parmenides theory of the One which cannot change makes it impossible to understand a universe where changes are indeed observed. Though Parmenides called these mere illusions, one has to account for them anyway. A single element world is automatically ruled out by Parmenidean logic. This leads to a pluralistic world quite naturally. In other words, Empedocles agreed with Parmenides that no change could occur, but only if there is only a single basic element. By increasing the number of fundamental elements he showed that changes can be accounted for.

9. What were the divine names by which Empedocles referred to the basic elements?

In his book, *On Nature*, Empedocles says: "Hear first the four roots of all things: bright Zeus, life-bringing Hera, Aidoneus, and Nestis who with her tears makes springs well up for mortals." Zeus refers to Fire and Nestis for Water. Scholars have argued about the symbolism of the other two deities. Hera may be taken as standing for Earth as she is described as life-bringing. Hence Aidoneus must be for Air.

But some have interpreted them the other way around.

10. What was Empedocles' greatest achievement as an experimental scientist?

Empedocles was the first to establish, by means of an experimental technique, that air is a substance that exerts a force (pressure). He took a commonly used utensil which consisted of a small bowl with holes in the bottom and a thin long In neck, and submerged the bowl into a bucket of water, keeping the narrow opening at the top closed with a finger. No water could enter the bowl. Similarly, when the vessel contained some water, the water could not flow out through the holes in the bottom as long as the top was kept closed. On the other hand, when the top was left open, entry and exit of water through the bottom holes became quite easy. From these observations Empedocles concluded that atmospheric air must be exerting forces like any material lid; in other words, that air was behaving like a material substance. He thus made the major discovery that matter can exist not only in the solid and liquid forms, but also in an extremely tenuous form as air which is not directly visible.

11. What is another major significance of this discovery?

Empedocles had shown that it was possible, by ingenious and indirect means, for us to become aware of aspects of the physical world that are not revealed to us directly through our senses. This was thus the starting point of the enormous extensions of the range of human perceptions that were to be achieved by the scientific endeavor in future generations.

12. What is the view of some historians of science on this experimental work of Empedocles?

Some have argued that Empedocles probably did not do any actual experiment to this effect, but that he simply drew interesting and insightful consequences from what was commonly observed, even by children, who often used the clepsydra as a plaything. In other words, it would be rash to describe what ever Empedocles observed, or perhaps even did, as part of what a scientific investigator in our own times would call an experiment.

13. Why do competent scholars on these matters have such differences of opinion in their interpretations?

Differences of opinions arise from several factors in this context. We do not have all the original writings and documents at our disposal, and one has to depend on secondary sources for bringing the past back to life. Also, on the basis of their general investigations historians of science form definite views of history and their interpretations are generally in the framework of their particular philosophies. Thus those who wish to emphasize that the ancient Greeks had laid the foundations for all science would tend to interpret the available writings as proof that Empedocles had indeed done scientific experiments also.

Those who are convinced that science develops only in the context of practical needs and economic techniques try to related eve*ry* major scientific advance to this or that economic aspect of a society. Those who are inclined to believe that individuals rather than external circumstances mold history suggest rather the genius of the individual as the source of new insights. Those who refer only to recorded facts and documents may be closest to the truth, but the corresponding history, though factual, may not be so interesting.

14. What was Empedocles' theory of vision?

Empedocles developed an elaborate theory to explain how we see things. He believed that "the interior of the eye is (the element) fire, and around it are earth and air through which, being fine in texture, it penetrates like the light in lanterns..." He also taught some thing to the effect that visible bodies emanate luminous particles which meet the rays that come out of our eyes. This is what makes objects visible.

15. What major insight regarding light is Empedocles credited with?

According to Aristotle, Empedocles held the view that light takes a finite time to reach us from the sun. If we accept what Empedocles says about light, notes Aristotle, "we must assume a time when the sun's say was not yet seen but was still travelling in the middle of space." This was, no doubt, a great intellectual insight.

16. What does one mean by Empedocles' Cosmic Cycle?

According to a classic interpretation of Empedocles' writings, the world passes through four successive stages which repeat themselves: In the first stage or period *Love* reigns supreme. All the elements are fused together. In the second period *Strife* gradually enters the scene and begins to separate out the elements. In the third stage Strife has completely taken over, and the elements are all well separated. In the fourth and final period, Love re-enters the scene and little by little the elements are brought together again. When this is completed, one has reverted to the first stage, and the process is repeated. This is the idea behind the concept of the Cosmic Cycle of Empedocles. Scholars have not been agreement as to whether the present phase of the world corresponds to Empedocles' third or fourth stage.

17. Do all scholars accept the Cosmic Cycle idea as a correct interpretation of Empedocles' writings?

No. In fact, some scholars have questioned this classic interpretation. They claim that Empedocles did not have any such oscillating cosmic evolution in mind.

18. What do we know of Empedocles as a man?

Historians have gathered several interesting views from extant writings about Empedocles as a person. He is often portrayed as a rather pompous individual with a very serious face and long hair. According to some stories he could cure the sick by what may be called faith healing, he once brought a woman back to life after she was dead, and he performed other miracles as well. He is also known to have been interested in applying his knowledge and views of nature to practical ends. According to another story he diverted the waters of a stream flowing through a city through his engineering skills so as to curb the plague that was rampaging the city. Thus he was not just a theoretical scientist. Yet, he is also known to have believed in Orphic mysteries.

19. What are Orphic mysteries?

Orpheus was an ancient Greek hero who is said to have possessed extraordinary powers. His sacred writings gave rise to a religious cult in the 6th century BCE In the Orphic writings one finds belief in primeval gods: *Eros* (Love) and *Phanes* (Light). These are supposed to have arisen from the egg of *Chronos* (Time). Orphism became a rigid authoritarian religious movement tending towards ascetism.

20. How, according to Diogenes Laertius, did Empedocles die?

Diogenes reports that once, after Empedocles brought a dead woman back to life, a feast was held to celebrate the happy event. While the feast was going on, Empedocles stepped out, and was never to be seen again. According to another legend he gave himself up into the mouth of the volcano Etna, where upon the volcano threw out his golden sandals. Thus the miracle mongering scientist disappeared mysteriously.

21. Where can one read in greater detail about Empedocles' philosophical system?

D. O'Brien's *Empedocles' Cosmic Cycle* (1969) is a scholarly analysis of Empedocles' philosophy, based on the surviving fragments of his writings as well as on secondary sources. The book includes an extensive bibliography on the subject. In this work O'Brien notes: "Empedocles attempts to preserve Parmenides' insight into the nature of the one and yet to restore the sensible world to reality by making the one and the many exist in succession. In this way the many are not illusory, while the one retains many of the characteristics of Parmenides' sphere, without ever ceasing to be spatial.... Empedocles' system is not of succession simply, but of cyclic succession, i.e. primarily an alternation of the one and the many..." These lines summarize how Empedocles expanded on Parmenides' worldview.

22. Has the idea of a cyclic succession of phases in the evolution of the world been put forward in any other system of thought?

Yes. The concept of the *yuga* in ancient Indic thought also speaks of cyclic phases of the universe.

75

VIII

ANAXAGORAS OF CLAZOMENAE

1. Who was the first great Athenian philosopher?

Anaxagoras (500 BCE - 428 BCE) of Clazomenae, the Ionian who went to settle down in Athens, befriended the famous statesman Pericles, and introduced Ionian scientific thinking in that great city, was the first of the Athenian philosophers.

2. What was Anaxagoras' view of the structure of matter?

There is considerable scholarly difference of opinion on this question. However, it is fair to say that Anaxagoras believed in the continuum as far as matter is concerned. He held the view that matter can be divided and subdivided indefinitely, each small part being made up of an infinity of smaller parts. Indeed, he is regarded as one of the first early thinkers to grasp the significance of infinity. And his theory of this continuum arose in his efforts to answer Zeno's paradoxes. Anaxagoras thus stated that there is no such thing as the smallest of all entities.

3. What was Anaxagoras' view on the ultimate constituents of matter, i.e. his concept of the elements?

Anaxagoras believed that material substances cannot be separated out into simpler elements. Indeed, in his view "there are many things of all kinds in all the things that are being mingled, and seeds of all things with every sort of shapes and colors and flavors." This is in accordance with the idea of the indivisibility of matter into ultimate entities. "When it is impossible for there to be a smallest," he says, "nothing can become separated or by itself, but just as in the beginning so now all things are together. Everything contains many things, the larger and the smaller containing an equal number of the things that are being separated off."

4. What were some of Anaxagoras' other scientific ideas and investigations?

Anaxagoras spoke about atmospheric physics: He wrote on the causes of winds, holding the view that winds arise from the rare faction of air due to the sun, as also when "when things were burned and made their way to the vault of heaven and were carried off." He said that the cause of thunder and lightning is to be found in the heat that strikes the clouds. He

recognized the cause of eclipses as due to the shadows of the earth and
the moon. He was also one of the first to realize that moonlight is nothing more than reflected sunlight, an idea which Empedocles also held. He had a theory for the cause of earthquakes: the impact of the air above ground on the ground itself. He had theories for the origin of planets and stars, and even of life. According to some interpretations of his writings, Anaxagoras is also believed to have imagined the possibility of intelligent life in other parts of the universe. Most of all, in the true Ionian spirit, Anaxagoras attempted to explain many things in naturalistic terms.

5. What was Anaxagoras' idea of the Mind?

Anaxagoras is said to have started his book with the state ment: "All things were together, then Mind came and set them in order." He stated that the Mind is infinite and can exist independently of anything. Mind is said to have initiated motion. Mind is eternal. Mind is described by him as the finest and purest of all things. (Modern physicists may note that the Greek word used by Anaxagoras to say 'finest' is lepton: often used to described *very* fine things, such as spider's webs. But this was the first use of the *word* to describe some general aspect of the physical world.) This may suggest that he had a materialistic view of the Mind.

6. What was Anaxagoras' view of the sun and the stars?

Anaxagoras is reported to have stated that "the sun and the moon and all the stars are fiery stones carried round by the rotation of the aether." More specifically he described the sun as "a red hot mass many times larger than Peloponnesus."
mas

7. What was a consequence of such a teaching?

A consequence of this was that he angered the masses and the religious fanatics of the time. One Diopeithes apparently spoke out vehemently against such heretical ideas which do not recognize the divinity of celestial bodies. In his old age he was tried for impiety and convicted. Anaxagoras was thus the first of the scientists to be put on trial for propounding unorthodox views. He was certainly not the last.

8. What punishment did Anaxagoras suffer?

According to one tradition he was imprisoned, and he escaped. According to another , he was simply exiled, and he lived peace fully in Lampsacus where he initiated the

young into philosophy. As per his wish, the children of the city were given a holiday
in the month of his death.

9. What are some other stories are associated with the name of Anaxagoras?

Anaxagoras is known to have come from a very well-to-do home. But he had little interest in material wealth. Instead he devoted his life to science and philosophy. He is said to have remarked that the goal of life should be the investigation of the sun, the moon, and the heavens: a truly pure scientist!

He had a very matter--of-fact view on things. When his son died he merely said he knew he had not given birth to an immortal human being. When he was told that the court had condemned him to die he replied that nature had condemned all of us to that fate. Once he was criticized for not taking any interest in his own country, devoting as he did his time to the exploration of the heavens. He is said to have explained that he was in fact enormously interested in his country -and pointed to the heavens: implying that he considered himself as part of the whole universe. He wrote but one book, according to the authorities in the Alexandrine library.

IX
LEUCIPPUS AND DEMOCRITUS

1 Who was Leucippus?

Leucippus (5th century BCE) was a contemporary of Empedocles and Anaxagoras. He is regarded as the originator of the atomic theory of matter, but he was greatly overshadowed by his pupil and successor Democritus who alone is often mentioned as the proponent of the atomic theory in ancient times.

2 Where was Leucippus from?

Leucippus was originally from Miletus, and his thinking was like that of other Milesian philosophers. But he was also well versed in Eleatic philosophy. And he probably taught in Abdera.

3 What was the scholarly controversy surrounding Leucippus?

The very existence of Leucippus has been questioned by some scholars. It all arose from the writings of the influential philosopher Epicurus (341 B.C. - 270 B.C.) who had declared something to the effect that no one by that name even existed. After many centuries during which, on the basis of other commentators, the existence of Leucippus was taken for granted, the controversy was re-started in the 19th century by E. Rohde who echoed Epicurus' statement about the non-existence of Leucippus. Other scholars took up the question, and now it is generally

4. Who were some contemporaries of Leucippus?

Leucippus of Miletus, who flourished in the 5th century BCE, was a contemporary of Empedocles and Anaxagoras. He is regarded as the originator of the atomic theory of matter, but he was greatly overshadowed by his pupil and successor Democritus who alone is often mentioned as the proponent of the atomic theory in ancient times.

4. On what basis can we be sure of the existence of Leucippus?

On the basis of the writings of Aristotle and of Theophrastus both of whom state clearly that Leucippus originated the atomic theory. He has also been described as a contemporary of Anaximander. Epicurus is also known to be unreliable when he talks about his predecessors. And his statement of the non-existence of Leucippus may well be an idiomatic way of saying that he (Epicurus) did not care for the views of such a man.

5 What works are attributed to Leucippus?

Leucippus is said to have authored *Great World Systems* and *On Mind*. The famous statement in the second work is: "Nothing comes to be at random, but all things come for a reason and of necessity." This statement, reflecting complete determinism, is the only surviving quotation from Leucippus.

6. Who was Democritus?

Democritus (460 B.C. - 360 B.C.) of Abdera is the philosopher who is generally referred to as the originator of the atomic theory in the ancient world. He is said to have introduced the word *a-tomos*, meaning *indivisible thing*.

7. What was Democritus' conception of the atom?

Democritus regarded atoms as the ultimate constituents of all mater. They are extremely small and invisible, eternal and incompressible. They have no pores. The atoms of different substances differ in their form, as the letter A differs from the letter N; they differ in their arrangement, as AN differs from NA; and in their position, as N is not more than 2 held vertically. Our senses perceive atoms differently, hence the variety in the physical world. Physical properties of substances arise from differences in the forms, figures and positions of atoms. There are an infinity of atoms in the void (kenon) of infinite space. Light bodies have more void in them compared to heavy bodies. And the atoms are always moving.

8. What was Democritus' concept of the motion of atoms?

In the Democritan theory of atoms, the atoms are constantly in motion in void. They collide with one another and bounce back and move again. In the words of one ancient commentator, the atoms are not only moving all the time, but they also catch up "with one another," and collide, "whereupon some rebound at hazard and others become entangled." One sees here a remarkable
distant perception of the modern kinetic theory. Yet, as Aristotle complained, Democritus did not quite explain the origin of the atomic motions.

9. What physical principle (of modern science) is dimly implicit in Democritus' idea of atomic motions?

Democritus statement that "atoms have no weight, but they move by mutual impact in infinite space," has been interpreted by Santillana as "the earliest statement of the inertial principle." For in this proposition Democritus seems to distinguish clearly between weight and inertial mass.

10. What was Democritus' conception of soul atoms?

The atoms of soul are spherical, according to Democritus. They are distributed throughout the living body and are supposed to be endowed with a divine principle. These soul atoms continually interact with the atoms of the physical body. The various soul atoms give different attributed to the different parts of the body: reason to the head, desire to the liver, anger to the heart, etc. As long as there is life in the body, fresh atoms are inhaled. When the organism stops breathing, most soul atoms are squeezed out of the body, and death results. But some soul atoms may still remain in the body even after death. These are responsible for the continued growth of nails, hair, etc. even after death.

11. What was Democritus' conception of the world?

Democritus imagined the earth to be flat and elongated, its length being about one and a half times as much as its breadth. Initially the earth was not where it is now, having strayed about. But in course of time its thickness increased, it became heavier, and finally it came to rest at the center of the universe in a slightly tilted position.

The earth is stable in its position thanks to the air around it.

12. What was Democritus' view of chance in the physical world.

Democritus, like Leucippus and other atomists, was a strict determinist. He maintained that everything evolves in accordance with rigid causality. However, because of the enormous complexity of the physical world, because of the very large number of components, the possibilities also increase enormously. This makes it difficult for us ordinary humans to trace all the myriad causal links. As a result, becasue of our own ignorance and limited capacities, some events may seem to us to result from pure chance. Thus Democritus was expressing a view that was to be elaborated and enunciated many generations later in the 19th century by Laplace.

13. What were some other subjects on which Democritus wrote?

According to Diogenes Laertius, Democritus wrote some seventy-two works in all on a wide variety of subjects. The topics included: mathematics, physics, astronomy, geography, music, medicine, philosophy, geography, art, navigation, psychology, and psychotherapy.

14. What are some of the famous sayings of Democritus?

"Verily we know nothing.' Truth is buried deep." "Culture is better than riches." "Strength of body is nobility only in beasts of burden; strength of character is nobility in man."

"Good actions are to be done, not from compulsion but from conviction; not from hope of reward, but for their own sake."

"Many much-learned men have no intelligence." "Man is universe
in little."

"I alone know that I know nothing."

15. What was Democritus theory of enthusiasm?

Literally the word *enthusiasmos* meant *God within us*. Democritus suggested that enthusiasm *was* a state in which the soul atoms were possessed by God. This was an interesting blend of materialism and spiritualism, and *was* perhaps one of the
earliest attempts at a physical explanation for a state of mind.

16. What information do we have about Democritus's life?

Democritus came from Abdera, a place that had somehow acquired a reputation for producing not *very* intelligent people. He went to Athens and is said to have seen the great philosopher Socrates. He inherited a lot of wealth from his father and is known to have traveled great deal. He is said to have remarked: "Among my contemporaries I have traveled over the greatest portion of the earth in search of things the most remote, and have seen the most climates and countries, and heard the largest number of thinkers." It has been suggested that he visited not only Babylonia and Persia, but also India. Democritus was a man of good humor and cheer, and was sometimes referred to as the *Laughing Philosopher*.

17. What were the circumstances of Democritus' death?

According to one story, when Democritus became quite sick at the ripe old age of one hundred and nine, his sister was *very* concerned that he would die before an impending festivity in which she was involved. He is said to have assure her that this would not happen. And not long after the said festivities Democritus apparently died peacefully. His secret for longevity, according to one report, was daily baths in oil and eating plenty of honey.

18. In which other philosophic tradition was the atomic theory developed?

A detailed and complex atomic theory was developed by Indian thinkers from the sixth century BCE on. The basic idea was that the material world is ultimately made up of *paramánus* : ultimate atoms, the objects of everyday experience being merely aggregates of these primordial atoms. Our senses endow these aggregates with the properties of taste, smell, etc. In India there arose several competing versions of the atomic theory in the course of the centuries.

19. Could Democritus have been influenced by Indian atomism?

By the close of the 19th century R. Garbe, a scholar who had examined the question at some length after a thorough study of classical Indian philosophies, commented in one of his studies: "The historical possibility of the Grecian world of thought being influenced by India through the medium of Persia must unquestionably be granted, and with it the possibility of ... ideas being transferred from India to Greece." However, this view is not shared by other (modern) scholars, especially those scholarly commitments have been to Greece and to Western science. George Sarton, referring to views such as Garbe's, writes: "...such assumptions are unproved and gratuitous... The Greeks were quite capable of reaching that solution (atomic theory to answer some metaphysical questions) by themselves, and so were the Hindus."

20. Where can one read more on Democritus' theory and its impacts?

One may consult C. Bailey, The Greek Atomists and Epicurus (1928). In this book the author has this to say on Democritus: "Democritus was neither a skeptic, nor a rationalist, nor a phenomenalist, he does not fit into any of the modern categories; he neither denied nor affirmed the truth of all sensation nor of all thought, but built for himself a "theory of knowledge," subtle and almost paradoxical, but based directly on his atomic conception of the world. The final realities of the universe, the atoms and the void, are real and are capable of being known by the mind. Phenomena are built up of the final realities and retain the primary properties of size and shape: as such they are real and can be known by the senses." Here we see one of the fundamental assumptions required in building the scientific edifice. Any worldview that doubts or rejects this possibility of comprehending an external reality in terms of the human mind automatically dilutes any enthusiasm for scientific exploration, although such a view may *well* be logically sound and metaphysically fruitful.

91

X
BRIEF END-NOTE

Pre-Socratics and Ionia

Because of the wealth of materials that has been accumulated on ancient Greece, and because of its significance and lasting impact on later science, this chapter is longer than the others. It will therefore be divided into three broad sections. The first will consider Greek thought in the Pre-Socratic period, between 600 and 450 BCE.

The first flickers of European science is said to have begun in a narrow strip on the coast of the Mediterranean Sea. A thousand years before the dawn of the Christian era, settlers from mainland Greece, driven, it is believed, by the Dorians, made their homes in the region which also included a number of islands. Twelve major cities were thus established: Miletus, Myus, Priene, Ephesus, Kolophon, Lebdus, Teos, Erythrae, Klazomenae, Phocaea, Samos, and Chios. All these were part of what came to be known as Ionia.

New political institutions were formed. As yet there were no heavy traditions of long centuries. Fresh thinking and new perspectives were thus natural and uninhibited. There also existed a thriving commerce with alien shores, resulting in a continual intermingling of peoples with different interests and diverse backgrounds.

Such interactions always open up new ways of thinking and imaginative reactions to strange ideas. Many practical needs also arose, instigating search for solutions to problems encountered never before. All this provided ample opportunities for careful investigation, serious reflection, and original thought.

Thus it was in Ionia that the pre-Socratic thinkers first arose. Their thinking was not entirely independent of Egyptian and Babylonian ideas with which many of them were familiar. But they injected into them newer visions, and encouraged an approach that was to bear much fruit in the generations to follow.

The sources

Modern historians owe much to the writers of ancient times who have left comments and anecdotes relating to the ancients who have gone without a trace. Among such ancient writers who have served us in this way, let us mention five.

First there was Herodotus (5th century BCE) who is regarded in the Western tradition as the first of all historians. His writings have provided us with a fund of information on various aspects of the ancients. The word history is derived from the Greek *istorie* which simply meant inquiry. It was Herodotus who first used it in the sense of inquiry into the past. It is said that he used to read his historical writing to the public in Athens and in Olympia. Herodotus also realized how difficult it is to be absolutely certain about one's statements in this context. "My business is to record what people say," he is reputed to have declared, "But I am not obliged to believe it all."

Then there was Aristotle (4th century BCE). He was the great scientist-philosopher of ancient Greece whom we shall consider in some detail later. He too has left behind numerous references to earlier thinkers.

Theophrastus (4th century BCE) was an associate of Aristotle. He was a philosopher too, and did work on botany. His own work led to a classification of thinkers in accordance with their opinions, which came to be known as the doxographical tradition. Theophrastus's writings are an important source of information.

Plutarch (1st - 2nd century CE) wrote a book called *Parallel Lives* which gives a number of (traditionally accepted) facts about the various thinkers we will be mentioning in this chapter.

Finally there was Diogenes Laertius (3rd century CE). He has left behind a history of Greek thought which has been widely used by modern scholars to gather information on ancient philosophers. This work was first published in English in 1853 with the title *Lives and opinions of eminent philosophers*. The work is filled with interesting details, not all of which are reliable.

These, then, are the principal sources of our knowledge of ancient Greek science. A considerable amount of modern scholarship on the subject has grown from these apparently limited sources. Amplification and reinterpretation of these have been growing in volume and vigor, as well as arguments and counter-arguments as to the content and degree of alien influences on Greek philosophy.

RHYMES ON PRE-SOCRETIC SCIENCE

The spark of science, some once thought,
By the ancient Greeks first was caught.
That isn't what we'd now state,
But those Greeks were still quite great.

Their science and glory first began
By the genius of a single man.
Thales was this thinker's name
He's attained a lasting fame.

His sweeping words still strongly ring:
"From water comes just everything."
This line is great for it affirms
What Nature is, in physical terms.

Thales studied angles right,
And circles, and the stars at night.
But he also knew when his native soil,
Would yield rich harvest for olive oil.

When the Lydians in a battle met
The Persians, a dark eclipse set.
Thales had this event foretold
In those distant, distant days of old.

Anaximander was another Greek;
The cause of the world he liked to seek.
From apeiron, he boldly told,
Came a seed of hot and of cold.

He also made a circular chart
Of our world, and at its heart,
His beloved Hellas was put in place
With ethno-centric lack of grace.

Anaximenes was also there.
For him the cause of all was just the air.
When tiny bits of air condense,
We get water, earth and all substance.

Now here's what to science these bring:
They view not Nature as a godly thing.
This godless vision was handed to us
From the island thinkers of Miletus.

Once in Samos there truly was
A mystic man called Pythagoras.
His theorem on the hypotenuse
Does some people still confuse.

A magic-mongering man was he
Who saw mathematics in harmony
He did on souls and symbols write
On portents shed some ancient light.

He formed a secret society
Whose members frowned on levity.
They were against all loud laughter.
We know not what they were really after.

They were against a very wide street.
They said one should never eat meat.
They avoided the eating of any bean.

And they were in the public rarely seen.

Heraclitus' theory of opposite tensions,
Tells us how this world oft functions:
Changes, he said, do come about
When balance between tensions is out.

Heraclitus was a man of much ire,
To him the root of all was a central fire.
Another thing he firmly says:
"Everything flows, and nothing stays."

He was also quite a haughty man,
In his old age to a mountain he ran.
Ate grass and plants, such things he tried.
Under a heap of dung at last he died.

Xenophanes expressed the definite view
That the world was never something new,
And the universe has been for e'er sublime,
Since there was in fact no start for Time.

For him the earth really meant
Another basic element.
Of God, he said, no one can say
Anything certain, try one may.

Parmenides wrote a poem the Sun;
Said different things are truly One;
The One as many appears to be,
But this without knowledge one can't see.

Parmenides' pupil Zeno brought
Paradox to the field of human thought:
When there are opposing statements two,
And both seem to be equally true.

Empedocles, he surely was
The great philosopher of Acragas.
This serious man, it has been said
Revived a woman who had been dead.

He spoke of love and of hate
As the principles which create
Changes in things which at their core
Are made of elements in number four.

This pompous man with very long hair
Showed that pressure was caused by air.
But of light this is what he says:
That from our eyes come visible rays.

Anaxagoras to Athens went;
His productive years, there he spent.
He wrote on the moon, and on lightning,
On winds, and on many a thing.

He thought the sun which brightly shone
Was just a piece of red hot stone.
The finest thing that you ever can find,
He said, it was the human mind.

His life was filled with milk and honey
But he cared not a jot for all his money.
They said to his country he was a curse

He said that country was the universe.

He said the world wasn't just for us,
They said he was very impious.
Condemned to die he simply said, "Why,
But Nature has condemned all to die!"

From Abdera came Democritus
A name well known to many of us
As the one who first boldly swore
That atoms are in matter's core,

That moving atoms never pause,
That for everything there is a cause.
That atoms are of different kinds,
Controlling actions, hearts, even minds.

He was cheerful, he was wise.
He laughed a lot, traveled likewise.
He was a man who had no fears,
He lived to be a hundred years.

These were some of the early sages
Whose names and thoughts fill the pages
Of what is sometimes said to be
Pre-Socratic Science history.